The Japanese Kitchen

The Asian Testkitchen

Published by Mindful Publishing

TABLE OF CONTENT

Japanese steak rolls

Onigiri with tuna - mayonnaise - filling

Onigiri with salmon and chicken

Miso soup

Japanese cold buckwheat noodles with dip

Omuraisu

Japanese green tea - ice cream

Grilled salmon

Soba noodles with sesame and soy sauce

Ginger - soy sauce

Teriyaki - Sauce

Japanese sesame dressing

Miso soup with vegetables and tofu

Sushi salad

Japanese curry with beef

THE ASIAN TESTKITCHEN

Radish salad

Sushi

Okonomiyaki Osaka style

Yakitori

Spinach salad with sesame dressing

Gyoza

Quick miso ramen

Hokkaido Milk Bread

Sushi - Rice

Tamagoyaki - Japanese omelet

Japanese melon rolls

Green beans with sesame dressing

Japanese noodles with mushrooms

Nori-Maki sushi filling Mushrooms

Pak Choi soup with chicken

Japanese Lemon Chicken

Red - Beans - Paste

Beef Stir Fry with Udon Noodles

Katsudon

Okonomiyaki

Sukiyaki

Sesame cream with sugar syrup

Japanese seaweed salad

Baked chicken with Japanese sauce

Maki

Fried udon noodles with beef

Chicken Teriyaki

Japanese grilled salmon with teriyaki sauce

Japanese noodle soup with chicken broth and sirloin - ramen

O - Yakodon

Ichigo Daifuku

Crispy chicken schnitzel with curry sauce

Anpan

Udon noodles with tofu and spinach in pepper sauce

JAPANESE STEAK ROLLS

Working time approx. 25 minutes
Rest period approx. 30 minutes
cooking / baking time approx. 10 minutes
Total time approx. 1 hour 5 minutes

ingredients
500 g steak or fillet
16 asparagus, green, peeled
16 spring onion(s)
6 tablespoons rice wine, spiced
6 tablespoons soy sauce
4 teaspoons of sugar
1 tablespoon of oil (sesame oil)

Preparation
Cut the steak into 16 strips (about 1 cm thick) and beat them 0.5 cm thin. Put an asparagus and a green onion on top of the meat and roll it over both. Hold it together with a wooden toothpick.
Do the same with the rest of the meat, asparagus and green onion. Place them next to each other on a bak-

ing tray.

Mix the remaining ingredients (rice wine, soy sauce, sugar and sesame oil) and pour it over the steak rolls (for 30 minutes).

Then grill everything for 5-7 minutes and put the rolls on a plate. Pour the marinade through a sieve into a small pot and boil it for about 5-10 minutes until the marinade thickens a bit. Pour it over the rolls with a spoon.

Instead of asparagus and green onions you can also use peppers, zucchini or mushrooms.

It tastes good hot or cold. You can also cut the finished rolls into small pieces and serve with rice and Japanese cucumber salad.

ONIGIRI WITH TUNA - MAYONNAISE - FILLING

Working time approx. 40 minutes
cooking / baking time approx. 20 minutes
Total time approx. 1 hour

ingredients
250 g rice (sticky rice)
Tin of tuna
1 tablespoon mayonnaise
Nori leaves
Water
Salt
possibly wasabi paste

Preparation
Wash the sushi rice until the water is clear and prepare according to the instructions on the packet. If you have a rice stove, put the rice in it and add as

much water as you need until a part of your index finger fits between the rice and the water. Add a little salt to the water.

In the meantime, drain the tuna and mix it with mayonnaise and wasabi (very spicy) according to taste. Prepare a small bowl (like a cereal bowl) with a teaspoon of salt. Cut the nori leaf (best with scissors) into 6 equal strips.

When the rice is ready, spread it out on a plate and let it cool down to about 40 degrees. Moisten your hands with the prepared salt water and take a good handful of rice in your hand. Press a small hole in the middle with your thumb to fill in a teaspoon of the tuna-mayonnaise mixture. Cover it with rice and moisten your hands again and again so that the rice does not stick to it. Form the rice into a triangle in your hand. Put one of the nori stripes around one of the three sides to get a better grip on the onigiri.

Serve the onigiri warm (they cool down quickly, but are just as delicious when cold!).

ONIGIRI WITH SALMON AND CHICKEN

Total time approx. 30 minutes

ingredients
2 cup/s of rice (round grain rice)
100 g salmon, smoked, or very fresh
100 g chicken breast fillet
2 nori leaves
3 tablespoons vinegar (Sushi-zu), already prepared Sushi vinegar to season the rice
Wasabi paste
Soy sauce, for dipping
mayonnaise at will
according to taste spice mixture (Furikake-)

Preparation
Rinse the round grain rice well in a sieve until the water remains clear. Pour into a pot with 4 cups of water. Bring the rice to a boil over high heat. As soon as foam starts to rise in the pot, turn off the heat and

let the rice rest for 15 minutes on the hot plate. Very important: While the rice is cooking and afterwards never take off the lid. The best way to find out when the rice is boiling is to use a pot with a glass lid.
Season the still hot rice with the sushi and let it get cold.

In the meantime, dice the chicken breast fillet, season it and fry it. Dice the salmon. Cut each nori leaf into 5 equally sized strips.

Now form balls from the rice. The easiest way is to use an onigiri form, which is available in different shapes and sizes. Fill the rice balls in the middle with salmon or chicken. If you like, add a dab of mayonnaise to the filling.

Spread the finished onigiri with some wasabi paste and wrap each with a strip of nori.

MISO SOUP

Total time approx. 10 minutes

ingredients
600 ml water
1 teaspoon fish stock, instant - Dashi powder, alternatively a few (!) vegetable stock cubes
3 tablespoons of spice paste (miso, soybean paste) - available in different flavors in Asian or organic stores
1 spring onion(s), cut into thin rings
as desired Tofu, diced, diced potatoes, diced radish, bean sprouts, onions, leaf spinach, wakame (seaweed)

Preparation
Bring water to the boil, stir in dashi powder.
Pour miso into a small bowl and stir with a little dashi broth until smooth.
Miso easily forms lumps when added directly to the broth!
It is best to mix it with an egg whisk in a separate bowl or - true to style as in Japan - you put the miso in a ladle and gradually add more and more broth while stirring :-)

Finally bring the broth to the boil again with the miso.

Depending on the mixture, add the tofu, potatoes, carrots, radish and bean sprouts, then divide the soup into small bowls into which the spring onion rings have been placed.

JAPANESE COLD BUCKWHEAT NOODLES WITH DIP

Working time approx. 20 minutes
Rest period approx. 30 minutes
Total time approx. 50 minutes

ingredients
600 g noodles (soba, Japanese buckwheat noodles)
4 spring onion(s)
1 nori leaves
possibly wasabi paste, Japanese, green, from a tube or powder
For the sauce:
1 ½ cup/s of water
0,33 cup/s of sake, alternatively white wine or mild sherry
1 tablespoon of sugar
0.33 cup/s of soy sauce, Japanese

0.33 teaspoon Dashi, Japanese instant fish broth

Preparation

Bring all the ingredients for the dip briefly to the boil, then simmer for 2-3 minutes at low heat. Cool in a water bath and then place in the refrigerator for at least 30 minutes.

Cut spring onions into fine rings. If available, cut nori into thin strips with scissors.

Boil soba in plenty of boiling water according to package instructions, then put into a sieve and quench ice-cold. Rinse well, then drain.

Put the noodles in 4 plates (sprinkle Nori strips over them if necessary), spread the sauce in 4 dipping bowls.

Mix spring onions and wasabi (hot!) in the dip sauce and dip the noodles (chopsticks for chopsticks or fork for fork) briefly in the sauce. A typical summer meal in Japan. And in true style, soba is of course sipped audibly.

OMURAISU

670 kcal
Working time approx. 30 minutes
cooking / baking time approx. 20 minutes
Total time approx. 50 minutes

ingredients
8 eggs
400 g chicken breast, finely diced
4 mushrooms, or shiitake mushrooms
1 medium sized onion(s)
300 g rice, ready cooked, e.g. a rest
2 tablespoons soy sauce
1 garlic clove(s)

For the sauce:
2 tablespoons tomato paste
2 tablespoons of sugar
2 tablespoons soy sauce
2 tablespoons vinegar
½ teaspoon of allspice, or clove powder
to taste tomato ketchup
Cayenne pepper

Also:

salt and pepper
Oil, for frying

Preparation

Marinate the chicken in 2 tablespoons of soy sauce for a quarter of an hour. Finely dice onion and finely chop or crush garlic clove. Cut mushrooms into fine slices. Sauté onion in a little oil, add mushrooms, garlic and chicken and fry until the meat is lightly browned. Season to taste with salt and pepper. Then mix in the pre-cooked rice and put aside.

Mix a tomato sauce from the remaining soy sauce, tomato paste, sugar, vinegar and a teaspoon of salt, season with pimento or cloves and a little cayenne pepper and bring to the boil briefly or use the appropriate amount of tomato ketchup instead. Add half of the sauce to the meat-rice mixture.

Stir two eggs briefly in each case (do not beat), salt them and put them in a coated pan with a little oil. When the omelette is firm at the bottom and just stiff at the top, put some meat-rice mixture in the middle, form an oval shape and beat the ends together over the middle. It should look like a baseball. Then slide it over the edge of the pan and put it on a plate with the omelette edges facing down. Paint snake lines on the omelettes with the remaining tomato sauce.

JAPANESE GREEN TEA - ICE CREAM

211 kcal
Working time approx. 10 minutes
Rest period approx. 1 hour
Total time approx. 1 hour 10 minutes

ingredients
½ liters of cream
½ Liters of milk
175 g sugar
1 pinch(s) of salt
17 g tea, green powdered tea (Matcha)

Preparation
Stir all ingredients together until the sugar has dissolved.

Freeze in the ice cream machine. (Takes about 30-40 min.)

The ice cream will probably not freeze completely in the ice-cream maker (since it does not contain eggs). Therefore, simply place it in the freezer again for 30-60 minutes afterwards, then it has a nice consistency and is ready to eat.

GRILLED SALMON

Working time approx. 10 minutes
Rest period approx. 1 hour
cooking / baking time approx. 3 minutes
Total time approx. 1 hour 13 minutes

ingredients
1 lemon(s) (Yuzu, Japanese lemon), alternatively lime or lemon
80 ml soy sauce, Japanese
80 ml Mirin (rice wine, Japanese) sweet
80 ml Sake (rice wine, Japanese)
8 slice/s of salmon fillet, 50 g each

Preparation
Rinse yuzu or lime (lemon) well under hot water, then cut into 4 slices.
Mix the soy sauce, mirin and sake in a bowl. Place the salmon slices in a bowl and pour the marinade over them. Spread the lemon slices over the salmon. Cover the salmon in the marinade and leave to marinate in the refrigerator for at least 1 hour.
Take the salmon out of the marinade, dab it dry and fry (grill) it in a pan or on the barbecue for about 3 min.

SOBA NOODLES WITH SESAME AND SOY SAUCE

Working time approx. 20 minutes
Rest period approx. 10 minutes
cooking / baking time approx. 10 minutes
Total time approx. 40 minutes

ingredients
2 tablespoons sesame oil
2 tablespoons soy sauce, light
2 tablespoons Mirin
6 Shiitake mushroom, dried
250 g soba noodles (Japanese buckwheat noodles)
6 spring onion(s)
5 cm ginger root, fresh
2 clove(s) of garlic
1 tablespoon sesame, roasted
200 ml water, boiling
Mint leaves to garnish

Preparation

Mix 1 tablespoon of sesame oil with the soy sauce and mirin to a dressing. Cut spring onions lengthwise into thin strips of 5 cm. Cut ginger into thin strips. Cut garlic into thin slices.

Pour 200 ml boiling water over the mushrooms in a bowl and soak for 10 minutes. Pour off, collecting 100 ml soaking water. Remove the woody mushroom stalks and cut the hats into strips.

Cook the noodles in boiling water for 3 minutes, drain.

Heat the remaining oil in a wok over medium heat, add the spring onions, ginger and garlic and stir for 2 minutes. Add mushrooms and noodles, heat while stirring, then add the sesame dressing and the mushroom water. Coat the noodles with the sauce while stirring.

Sprinkle the dish with sesame seeds and garnish with mint.

GINGER - SOY SAUCE

Total time approx. 15 minutes

ingredients
20 g ginger - root
½ teaspoon chili pepper(s), red
4 clove/s of garlic, pressed
100 ml soy sauce, Japanese
8 tablespoons vinegar (rice or white wine vinegar)
8 tablespoons rice wine or sherry, dry
2 tablespoons of sugar
1 tablespoon of oil (sesame oil)

Preparation
Peel the ginger root, remove the seeds from the chillies. Cut both into fine cubes and put them in a pan with the garlic. Add soy sauce, vinegar, rice wine or sherry, sugar and sesame oil, mix well and heat. Reduce the sauce by half. Ready. Goes well with meat or fried fish.

TERIYAKI - SAUCE

Working time approx. 15 minutes
cooking / baking time approx. 1 hour
Total time approx. 1 hour 15 minutes

ingredients
220 g sugar, brown
100 g ginger, fresh
50 g garlic clove(s)
3 orange(s)
200 ml soy sauce, light

Preparation
Put the brown sugar in a pot and let it caramelize slightly. Then peel the ginger and cut into fine strips. Now peel the garlic and cut it into fine strips as well. Rinse the oranges with hot water and rub the peel into fine strips with a zest ripper and then squeeze the oranges. Add the ginger and garlic to the caramelized sugar and sweat lightly in it. Then add the orange zests and steam briefly. Deglaze with 200 ml orange juice and the soy sauce and simmer everything for about 1 hour on a low heat.

Goes well with short-fried tuna, prawns and

chicken.

JAPANESE SESAME DRESSING

500 kcal
Total time approx. 10 minutes

ingredients
2 tablespoons of water, or dashi broth
2 tablespoons sesame, white
2 tablespoons sesame paste
1 tablespoon soy sauce, Japanese
1 tablespoon of rice vinegar, or other neutral vinegar
1 tablespoon of sugar

Preparation
Briefly toast the sesame seeds in a pan without oil and then lightly crush them in a mortar. Then mix with sesame paste, water, soy sauce, vinegar and sugar.

Pour over the salad.
A good salad is lettuce with carrots.

MISO SOUP WITH VEGETABLES AND TOFU

195 kcal
Total time approx. 25 minutes

ingredients
1 large carrot(s)
1 stick/s of leek (thin stick)
200 g mushrooms (shiitake, age-old oyster mushrooms)
250 g tofu
1 tablespoon of oil
900 ml vegetable broth
2 tablespoons spice paste (Miso-Paste, Asia-Shop)
1 bunch of chives
salt and pepper

Preparation
Peel and slice the carrot lengthwise into thin strips, then cut crosswise into fine strips. Wash the leeks and cut into fine strips. Rub the mushrooms clean

and cut them into strips. Cut the tofu into small cubes.

Heat the oil in a soup pot and fry the mushrooms for about 2 minutes while stirring. Pour the vegetable stock over the mushrooms and add the prepared vegetables. Simmer open at medium heat for about 3-4 minutes until the vegetables are firm to the bite. Now stir the miso paste into the soup and add the tofu. Let it simmer in the soup at low heat for 2 minutes. Season to taste with salt and pepper. Cut the chives into fine rolls and sprinkle them on the soup. Serve hot.

SUSHI SALAD

Working time approx. 30 minutes
Rest period approx. 30 minutes
cooking / baking time approx. 15 minutes
Total time approx. 1 hour 15 minutes

ingredients
100 g sushi rice, dry
150 ml water
25 ml rice vinegar
1 tablespoon of sugar
Salt
120 g shrimp(s), pre-cooked
100 g salmon, raw, fresh or frozen
1 cucumber(s)
3 nori leaves (roasted seaweed)
1 tablespoon ginger, pickled, drained
2 lime(s)
½ teaspoon wasabi paste
1 tablespoon soy sauce
1 tablespoon sweet chili sauce

Preparation
Wash the rice and simmer gently in a pot covered with water for 15 minutes (add more water if neces-

sary), remove from heat and let it swell for another 30 minutes.

Mix rice vinegar, 1 teaspoon of sugar and 1/4 teaspoon of salt and add to the rice.

Peel the cucumber, remove the seeds and cut into small cubes. Cut nori leaves into small pieces (best done with kitchen scissors). Cut the salmon into small pieces as well. Then carefully mix everything - including the prawns and ginger - with the cooled rice.

Squeeze the limes. Mix wasabi, lime juice, soy sauce and sweet chili sauce and the remaining sugar and mix this dressing with the salad. Chill again and let it soak through.

Do not store the salad for long, as raw salmon is included.

JAPANESE CURRY WITH BEEF

382 kcal
Total time approx. 40 minutes

ingredients
400 g goulash (beef), diced 1 cm
400 g potato(es), diced 1cm
200 g bell bell pepper(s), red, finely diced
200 g onion(s), halved, cut into strips
150 g mushrooms (Egerlinge), in strips
150 g carrot(s), halved lengthwise, striped crosswise
2 tablespoons curry powder
2 ½ tablespoon flour (heaped tablespoon)
800 ml broth
1 clove/n garlic
1 teaspoon ginger powder
1 teaspoon cumin, ground
at your discretion Cayenne pepper
2 teaspoons lemon juice
Oil for frying
salt and pepper

Preparation

After everything is peeled and cut, the ingredients should be sorted according to cooking time and distributed on 3 plates:

Dice of paprika and Egerlinge on one plate, carrots and potatoes on the second and the onions on the third plate. The meat is cut last and comes directly from Brett into the pot.

Put the oil in a medium high pot, covering it with oil. Heat up on highest level. When the oil is hot, add the meat and the clove of garlic. As soon as the meat is barely red, add the onions and reduce the heat a little (my stove goes from level 0.5 to level 3 - so at the beginning 3, then 2). As soon as the onions become glassy, add the curry powder and the ginger powder, mix well. Now add the carrots and potatoes, stir well once again, taking care not to burn in too much. After 2 to 3 minutes add the flour. Mix well, fry briefly and then add the stock in 3 to 4 portions. Stir well and remove the crust from the bottom of the pot. Simmer for about 15 minutes on low heat (level 1 in my case), stirring occasionally. Then add the diced peppers and the mushrooms. Stir and let it simmer for about 10 minutes. Now add the lemon juice, the ground cumin and the remaining ingredients to taste and stir.

The curry can now be served with rice (Japanese sticky rice is a good choice).

RADISH SALAD

Total time approx. 15 minutes

ingredients
1 radish, white, peeled, grated
4 tablespoons rice vinegar, or white wine vinegar
2 tablespoons cane sugar
1 pinch(s) of salt
1 teaspoon horseradish, freshly grated or 2 teaspoons hot from the glass
1 teaspoon juice (ginger juice)
¼ Cucumber(s), peeled, diced, (as desired)

Preparation
Squeeze the radish well between the paper towels and mix with the other ingredients.

Tip:
For the ginger juice, place a piece of unpeeled ginger root in the garlic press.

SUSHI

Total time approx. 50 minutes

ingredients
250 g rice (sticky rice, sushi - rice)
4 nori leaves
1 carrot(s), cut into thin strips
1 avocado, cut into thin strips
1 pack of surimi
as desired fish, fresh (e.g. tuna, salmon)
Wasabi paste
Ginger, pickled
½ teaspoon sugar
2 tablespoons vinegar (rice vinegar)
Soy sauce

Preparation
Rinse the sticky rice (sushi rice) well until clear water comes. Then cook as usual (package instructions). Put about half a teaspoon of sugar in two tablespoons of vinegar and heat it up. Slowly stir the warm vinegar into the still warm but ready cooked rice. The faster the rice cools down afterwards, the better it sticks later.

For Makisushi, place a nori leaf on a bamboo mat and spread a thin layer of sticky rice on it, so that about 3/4 of the leaf is covered with rice. Put a thin strip of carrot and avocado in the middle. Then add surimi or the fish of your choice. Roll everything up and cut across a few times.

For nigirisushi, make small piles of the rice and place the fish on top as a small fillet. If you like, you can also tie it up with thin nori strips.

Put it in the refrigerator until serving. Serve with soy sauce, pickled ginger and wasabi paste.

OKONOMIYAKI OSAKA STYLE

Working time approx. 20 minutes
cooking / baking time approx. 10 minutes
Total time approx. 30 minutes

ingredients
300 g flour (Okonomiyaki-)
2 eggs
water at will
½ White cabbage, depending on size
Sauce (Okonomiyaki-)
Mayonnaise, preferably Japanese
flakes (Bonito flakes or Katsuoboshi), fish flakes
Algae, seaweed (Aonori), dried
4 slices of bacon, wafer-thin, unsmoked, or 100 g seafood or mochi and grated cheese

Preparation
Mix one egg per person with the flour and water to a thin dough. Add water until the dough becomes slightly liquid. Fold the finely chopped white cabbage into the dough. The mixture should look as if

there is more cabbage than dough in it.
(Pickled pink ginger, leek and/or spring onions refine this even more).

Wet a heated pan with oil and fry meat, seafood or mochi (rice cakes, the simplest) in the pan for a short time. Now spread the dough over the filling like a round cake and fry well on both sides.
Make sure that the mochi are nice and soft before the dough comes on top and mix the cheese into them.

To serve, spread the okonomiyaki sauce, mayonnaise, aonori and katsuoboshi on the flat cake and the okonomiyaki is ready.

YAKITORI

Working time approx. 20 minutes
Rest period approx. 30 minutes
cooking / baking time approx. 15 minutes
Total time approx. 1 hour 5 minutes

ingredients
500 g chicken breast fillet
6 tablespoons of sugar
6 tablespoons Mirin
6 tablespoons sake
6 tablespoons soy sauce
2 tablespoons oil, (peanut oil)
15 g ginger
4 clove(s) of garlic
some spring onion(s)
1 handful of sesame

Preparation
Soak the wooden skewers in water for 20 minutes so that they do not burn during grilling. If you make yakitori in the grill pan, it is not necessary.

Wash and dry the chicken filet and cut it into cubes of about 3 cm. Cut the spring onions into about 10 cm pieces, also the green parts.

Finely chop the garlic cloves and ginger and put them with the sugar, mirin, sake, soy sauce and peanut oil in a blender jug and puree it properly with a hand blender until there are no pieces left. Then mix the sauce with the chicken meat and marinate for at least 30 minutes.

Fold the spring onion a few times so that it is as long as the chicken pieces and put them alternately on skewers.

Heat the rest of the marinade in a pot until it becomes a thick mush, then you won't taste the ginger so intensively. Put the skewers on the hot grill pan and fry them all around. Then turn them over again and again at medium heat for about 5 minutes and brush them with the marinade. The sugar should then create a nice glaze.

At the end sprinkle some sesame seeds over it and you are done.

SPINACH SALAD WITH SESAME DRESSING

153 kcal
Total time approx. 10 minutes

ingredients
250 g spinach, fresh
1 tablespoon sesame, roasted
1 tablespoon sesame paste (tahini)
2 tablespoons soy sauce, Japanese
2 teaspoons sugar
1 teaspoon vinegar (e.g. old master), or better Mirin
Water (salt water)

Preparation
Blanch the spinach in salted water and quench cold, then put it in a sieve and squeeze out more liquid after draining. Mix all the remaining ingredients in a bowl. Mix the spinach with dressing.

Serve with Sushi in small bowls and sprinkle with some additional sesame seeds.

GYOZA

Total time approx. 30 minutes

ingredients
For the filling:
200 g minced beef or mixed
1 small bunch of spring onion(s)
1 leek stick(s)
100 g Chinese cabbage
2 tablespoons soy sauce
1 teaspoon sesame oil
2 clove(s) of garlic
salt and pepper
Ginger, fresh, quantity to taste

Also:
Oil
1 package of dough sheets, (gyoza sheets from Asiashop)
Soy sauce

Preparation
Chop the Chinese cabbage, salt it and let it stand for about 10 minutes. Afterwards press out firmly. Cut the leek and spring onions into small, thin rings.

Chop or grate the ginger (depending on how rough you like it). Press the garlic through. Mix the minced meat well with all the ingredients, then season with salt and pepper, but be careful with the salt, because the soy sauce is also salty!

Lay out the goyza leaves and put a teaspoon of filling on each, fold and close well, just put small folds on the edge in not too big distances, this looks like ravioli.

Heat a pan with a little oil, place the gyozas in it and fry them. When they are brown at the bottom (don't leave them too light), pour water over them so that the gyozas are covered with water about halfway through. Cover the pan and cook the gyozas until the water is absorbed (don't worry, despite the lid the water is gone after a short time), this takes about 10 minutes.

Serve with soy sauce for dipping.

QUICK MISO RAMEN

Working time approx. 10 minutes
cooking / baking time approx. 20 minutes
Total time approx. 30 minutes

ingredients
1 onion(s)
2 clove(s) of garlic
1 piece ginger
soy sauce to taste
rice wine at your discretion, optional
2 liters of vegetable broth or chicken broth
as desired Miso paste, approx. 1 - 2 tablespoons
300 g Ramen noodles without egg
Oil for frying
For the topping:
1 spring onion(s)
some mushrooms, e.g. enoki, shiitake or porcini
250 g chicken breast
Sesame Oil
Chili Flakes
4 eggs

Preparation

Chop onion, ginger and garlic very finely and fry in a pot with a little oil. Deglaze with soy sauce and broth and bring to the boil. Add the miso paste - preferably through a small sieve, as it is difficult to dissolve. Season to taste with a little rice wine and soy sauce. The stock can be used directly or continue to simmer for 10 - 20 minutes.

Cook the noodles separately according to the instructions on the packet. Do not add to the broth.

Now prepare the toppings. Cut the spring onion. Clean and fry the mushrooms. Marinate the chicken breast, e.g. with soy sauce and oil, and fry. Boil the eggs for 7 minutes and then place them in iced water so that they are still nice and soft when served.

Place the pasta in the serving bowls. Then add the stock and spread the toppings on top. The toppings can be varied according to what you have at home.

HOKKAIDO MILK BREAD

Working time approx. 20 minutes
Rest period approx. 1 hour 30 minutes
cooking / baking time approx. 30 minutes
Total time approx. 2 hours 20 minutes

ingredients
For the pre-dough:
25 g wheat flour type 550
100 ml water

For the dough:
350 g wheat flour type 550
125 ml milk
½ cubes yeast, fresh
50 g sugar
2 packs vanilla sugar
½ teaspoon salt
1 egg
30 g butter, soft
1 lemon(s), slightly grated zest thereof
For brushing:

1 egg yolk
Milk

Preparation

Dissolve the flour in water and put the liquid in a small pot. Heat on the stove at low heat while stirring constantly until a pudding-like mass is formed. Set aside and let it cool down.

For the dough, place flour, sugar, vanilla sugar, salt, egg, butter and lemon zest in a bowl. Heat the milk and dissolve the yeast in it. Knead with the remaining ingredients and the cooled pre-dough for about 8 - 10 minutes. Cover the dough bowl with a kitchen towel and let it rest for about 45 minutes.

Dust the work surface and a rolling pin with flour. Form 4 equally sized portions of dough and roll out each portion to an elongated tongue with the rolling pin. Roll up the dough tongues from the short side. Place the 4 dough rolls with the seam facing down in a buttered and floured box form. Cover with a kitchen towel and let rest for 45 minutes. Brush the surface with a mixture of egg yolk and milk and bake at 175 degrees for 30 - 35 minutes.

SUSHI - RICE

237 kcal
Total time approx. 20 minutes

ingredients
250 g rice (sushi - rice)
2 tablespoons vinegar (rice vinegar)
1 tablespoon of sugar
1 teaspoon of salt

Preparation
Rinse the sushi rice in a sieve under cold running water until the water runs off clearly, and drain the grains well.

Bring the rice to the boil with 300 ml of water, boil for 2 minutes, reduce the heat, cover the rice and let it swell for 10 minutes at low heat.
Take off the lid, put 2 layers of kitchen paper between the pot and the lid and let the rice cool down for another 10 to 15 minutes.

In the meantime bring rice vinegar, salt and sugar to the boil and let it cool down again.
Pour the rice into a bowl, drizzle the spicy vinegar over it and fold it in with a wooden spatula, but do

not stir.

Cover the rice with a damp cloth until further use.

TAMAGOYAKI - JAPANESE OMELET

297 kcal
Working time approx. 15 minutes
cooking / baking time approx. 10 minutes
Total time approx. 25 minutes

Ingredients
4 eggs
1 teaspoon of mirin
2 teaspoons soy sauce
1 pinch(s) of salt
some sugar
some dashi powder, dissolved in 1 tablespoon of water
Oil

Preparation
Mix the eggs with dashi, soy sauce, salt, sugar, mirin (if there is no mirin, take more sugar). The egg should not become frothy.

Heat up a pan, preferably a rectangular one, rubbing it with oil. Add about 1/3 of the egg mixture to the pan. When the egg has set, carefully roll from one side towards the middle. Rub the free side of the pan with oil again and add some of the egg mixture. When the new layer of egg has set, roll again, this time from the other side of the pan towards the middle. Repeat these steps until the egg mixture is used up.

When the omelette is cooked, remove it from the pan and let it cool. Cut into strips on the narrow side and use for example for nigiri sushi.

JAPANESE MELON ROLLS

Working time approx. 40 minutes
Rest period approx. 2 hours
Total time approx. 2 hours 40 minutes

ingredients
For the yeast dough:
300 g flour
36 g sugar
5 g salt
200 ml water, warm
1 package dry yeast
30 g butter, room temperature

For the second dough:
80 g butter, room temperature
90 g sugar
80 g eggs, lightly whisked
200 g flour
1 teaspoon baking powder
some syrup, (melon syrup or other aromas)

Preparation

For the bread dough, sift flour, sugar and salt into a bowl and mix in the dry yeast. Then add the warm water, but not all at once, otherwise the dough may become too sticky. Knead until the dough no longer sticks to the base. When the dough is ready, you can knead in the butter. Knead until the dough does not stick anymore. Let the dough rise for about 1 hour in a warm place until it has doubled in volume.

During this time prepare the dough for the cover: Stir butter and sugar together until smooth. Then add the egg and the melon syrup or other flavours and stir well. Sieve the flour and baking powder and knead the dough. Form 12 small balls (35-40 g each) from this dough and put them in the refrigerator for half an hour.

Knead the risen bread dough again and form 12 dough balls from it. Roll out the 12 kneading dough balls from the refrigerator between 2 sheets of foil to form round plates and place a plate on each bread dough ball as a blanket. Make sure that the bread dough is not completely wrapped up, otherwise the blanket will tear when you go out for the second time. Sprinkle the blanket with sugar and either cut into it or decorate it with small cut-out pieces of dough.

Let the rolls rise for another 40 minutes and then place them in the preheated
Bake at 170 degrees for about 15 minutes.

GREEN BEANS WITH SESAME DRESSING

199 kcal
Total time approx. 15 minutes

ingredients
100 g beans, green
Saltwater
3 tablespoons sesame, white
1 tablespoon of sugar
1 teaspoon vegetable oil
1 teaspoon sesame oil
1 tablespoon soy sauce

Preparation
Cut off the ends of the beans, put them in boiling salted water for a few minutes until the desired bite strength is achieved. Then quench in cold water, dry very well and cut in half.

Roast the sesame seeds in a pan without adding oil for one or two minutes until roasted aromas develop. Then immediately crush it in a mortar. If the consistency is a bit like a paste (not too much!) and there are still pieces of sesame seeds in it, add the oil, soy sauce and sugar and mix.

Then mix the marinade with the beans. Goes well with fish!

JAPANESE NOODLES WITH MUSHROOMS

Working time approx. 20 minutes
cooking / baking time approx. 15 minutes
Total time approx. 35 minutes

ingredients
250 g Udon noodles
2 tablespoons sunflower oil
1 onion(s), red, cut into rings
1 clove/s of garlic, crushed
450 g mushrooms, mixed, e.g. shiitake, oyster mushrooms, brown mushrooms, ...
350 g Chinese cabbage, or Pak Choi
2 tablespoons sherry, sweeter
6 tablespoons soy sauce
4 spring onion(s), cut into rings
1 tablespoon sesame, roasted

Preparation
Place the pasta in a large bowl and pour boiling

water over it so that it is covered. Leave to soak for 10 minutes or according to package instructions. Then drain thoroughly.

Heat sunflower oil in a large wok. Add red onions and garlic to the wok and stir-fry for 2 - 3 minutes. Add the mushrooms and continue stirring for about 5 minutes until they are cooked. Add Chinese cabbage or pak choi, noodles, sherry and soy sauce to the wok. Mix all the ingredients and stir-fry for 2 - 3 minutes until the liquid boils up.

Place noodles with mushrooms in preheated bowls and sprinkle with spring onions and roasted sesame seeds.

NORI-MAKI SUSHI FILLING MUSHROOMS

Working time approx. 10 minutes
cooking / baking time approx. 30 minutes
Total time approx. 40 minutes

ingredients
4 mushrooms (Shiitak), dried
2 tablespoons soy sauce, Japanese
1 tablespoon of sugar

Preparation
Soak mushrooms in hot water for about 20 minutes. Remove stalks and cut the heads into fine strips. Let simmer in 1/2 cup of the soaking liquid together with the soy sauce and sugar until the liquid has almost evaporated. Allow to cool.

Work the mushroom strips into maki sushi (rice inner rolls). They look very good both in color (brown) and aroma (sweet, umami, sour) and form a nice contrast to vegetable stripes.

PAK CHOI SOUP WITH CHICKEN

242 kcal
Working time approx. 20 minutes
cooking / baking time approx. 13 minutes
Total time approx. 33 minutes

ingredients
150 g chicken breast fillet
200 g Pak Choi
1 carrot(s)
2 spring onion(s)
½ Onion(s)
1 garlic clove(s)
some ginger, peeled, grated
some chili pepper(s), without seeds
1 tablespoon sesame oil, light
600 ml vegetable broth or chicken broth, possibly a little more
½ Star anise
1 tablespoon soy sauce, plus something to season
some lemon juice
some sesame oil, dark

Pepper
Sugar

Preparation

Cut the chicken meat into strips. Clean and rinse the Pak Choi, remove the stalk, cut the stems and leaves into strips. Peel the carrot and cut it into thin strips with the julienne slicer. Clean and wash the spring onion and cut it into rings. Finely dice the peeled onion and garlic clove, chop the chilli pepper very finely.

Heat light sesame oil, fry onion, garlic, the white of the spring onion, pak choi stems and ginger. Deglaze with the broth. Add soy sauce, star anise and chili and simmer for eight minutes. Add chicken breast, carrot strips and Pak Choi green, cook for another three minutes. Season to taste with soy sauce, lemon juice, dark sesame oil, sugar and pepper, remove star anise. Serve sprinkled with the spring onion green.

JAPANESE LEMON CHICKEN

Working time approx. 30 minutes
cooking / baking time approx. 15 minutes
Total time approx. 45 minutes

ingredients
300 g chicken breast
1 egg white
½ teaspoon salt
some pepper

For the sauce:
1 lemon(s)
2 tablespoons honey
1 teaspoon of cornstarch
2 tablespoons soy sauce
2 tablespoons of water
Also:
30 g cornstarch
30 g flour
some sesame
lemon slice(s) as desired

Preparation

Cut the meat into approximately 2 cm pieces, put them in a bowl, add salt, pepper and the egg white and mix well. Let it stand for 10 minutes.

Squeeze the lemon and mix in a small bowl with the honey, water, soy sauce and a teaspoon of starch.

Add the flour and starch to the meat and mix well until the whole meat is well covered.

Heat oil in a frying pan or pot (just enough to cover about half of the meat) and cook the nuggets on both sides for about 3 minutes. Drain a little on kitchen paper or similar.

Stir the sauce mixture again and heat it in a pan until it thickens and add the nuggets and turn them in the sauce. To garnish, add some sesame seeds and lemon slices if necessary.

RED - BEANS - PASTE

Working time approx. 30 minutes
Rest period approx. 12 hours
Total time approx. 12 hours 30 minutes

ingredients
250 g beans, red (azuki)
250 g sugar
1 pinch(s) of salt

Preparation
Wash the beans quickly, soak in water overnight for shorter cooking times. Boil them in a pot with plenty of water, discard the water and boil the beans again with plenty of water. Add water from time to time and skim off the resulting foam more often. Simmer for about one to one and a half hours until the beans are cooked (try one bean while it is still firm to the bite, continue cooking).

Here you can also press the beans through a fine sieve and discard the skin to get a smoother paste (Japanese distinguish between Tsubuan, where you can still see whole beans, and Koshian, which is just smooth).

Then discard enough water so that the beans are just below the surface of the water. Add sugar and salt and cook for about 10 minutes at low heat. Then let the paste evaporate over high heat, stirring slowly with a wooden spoon. Remove from the heat when you can see the bottom of the pot while stirring.

BEEF STIR FRY WITH UDON NOODLES

Working time approx. 20 minutes
cooking / baking time approx. 10 minutes
Total time approx. 30 minutes

ingredients
2 large carrot(s), small diced
100 g sugar snap pea(s)
1 head broccoli, divided into florets
2 small shallot(s), in fine strips
2 packs Udon noodles (usually 200 g)
250 g fillet of beef (minute steaks) cut into strips
1 clove/n garlic, optional
at will Teriyaki sauce
as desired soy sauce, dark
oil (sunflower oil, rapeseed oil, sesame oil, which you have at hand)
pepper to taste
chili flakes at will
to taste roasted onions

Preparation

After the vegetables and meat are cut, cook the udon noodles according to the instructions on the packet and drain well.

Heat the oil in a frying pan. Fry the beef fillet strips in the pan until everything is browned (3 - 4 minutes), season with pepper to taste. Remove from the pan and set aside.

Fry carrots, broccoli, mangetout, onions (if you like, you can also add garlic, but not too early, otherwise it will be too brown) until the desired cooking level is reached. I like it even crispier and if the onions and carrots are cut into nice small pieces, it will take about 6 - 7 minutes.

Now add the udon noodles and the meat. Add Teriyaki sauce and dark soy sauce (about 2 - 3 tablespoons of each, but I always do it differently, just enough to have a little sauce everywhere) and mix everything.

Arrange everything on a plate and sprinkle with fried onions and chili flakes as you like. If you don't like fried onions so much, you can also cut spring onions into rings and sprinkle over them, or who wants both.

KATSUDON

Working time approx. 1 hour
cooking / baking time approx. 30 minutes
Total time approx. 1 hour 30 minutes

ingredients
200 g sushi rice or round grain rice
250 ml water, cold
4 pork cutlets or minute steaks
50 g Panko or breadcrumbs
2 eggs
2 spring onion stick(s)
3 tablespoons soy sauce
2 tablespoons Mirin
2 tablespoons sake (cooking sake)
200 ml Dashi or vegetable broth
salt and pepper
oil, neutral for frying

Preparation
Put the rice in a saucepan and wash it with cold water and one hand, drain the water and repeat several times (about 4-5 times) until the water is clear. Finally, add 250 ml of cold water so that the rice is slightly covered.

Bring the rice to the boil once on a high flame until it foams, then immediately turn off the heat and place the lid on the pot. Do not lift the lid for 20 minutes, but leave the rice to stand. Do not worry, nothing sticks.

In the meantime, wash the pork escalopes and pat them dry, whisk the egg on a flat plate, season it lightly with salt and pepper, put the panko on another plate.

Pull the pork escalopes through the egg one after the other and then roll them in the panko from both sides. Press the Panko well and distribute evenly on all sides. Unlike the Wiener Schnitzel, no flour is used here.

Fry the pork schnitzels one after the other in a pan with hot oil and drain them on a plate with kitchen paper.

Tip: You can tell when the oil is hot enough by holding a wooden spoon with the end in it and small bubbles form on the wood. Don't save on the oil, the cutlets must be at least halfway through (according to the thickness of the meat), otherwise they will bake and burn!

Cut the escalopes into bite-sized pieces and keep them warm in the oven at about 80 - 100 °C on a plate with kitchen paper at top and bottom heat.

Cut the spring onions into rings. Bring dashi, mirin, soy sauce and sake to the boil in a large pan over medium heat. Add the cutlets cut into strips.

Whisk the 2nd egg and add it after about 2 minutes, reducing the heat considerably (to level 1 or 2, depending on the stove). Finally, sprinkle the spring onions on top and cook for another 2 minutes. The egg should now have set and the cutlets should have absorbed the liquid well from the bottom.

Carefully turn the rice in the pot once with a moistened wooden spoon and put half of it on deep plates. Place the escalopes with the sauce/egg mixture on top and serve warm.

OKONOMIYAKI

Working time approx. 15 minutes
cooking / baking time approx. 10 minutes
Total time approx. 25 minutes

ingredients
300 g flour
210 ml water
2 eggs
4 large cabbage leaves (white cabbage)
Meat, different kinds
topping ingredients of your choice, e.g. mushrooms, seafood, chopped meat
Fat for frying

Also:
Bonito flakes (katsuobushi) at will
at will seaweed, dried (Aonori)
mayonnaise at will
sauce to taste (Okonomi sauce)

Preparation
Cut about four large, outer, green cabbage leaves without the hard, white leaf rib into thin strips, about 4 mm wide.

Mix the water, flour, eggs and the sliced cabbage.
You can now add other ingredients to the dough, e.g. seafood cut into small pieces, chopped meat or mushrooms, just as you wish.

Fry the dough like a pancake in a frying pan. The okonomiyaki should have a diameter of about 20 cm.

Before you turn the okonomiyaki over, you can put more ingredients into the still soft dough.
Then fry the okonomiyaki from the second side.

When fried, pour katsuobushi, aonori, mayonnaise and okonomi sauce over the okonomiyaki and serve.

SUKIYAKI

Total time approx. 30 minutes

ingredients

800 g beef (e.g. entrecôte), cut as thin as ham (!) at the butcher

1 tofu in cubes (solid tofu, soaked in cold water for 30 min and drained)

1 pack of glass noodles (blanched, quenched, drained and cut into small pieces with scissors)

400 g mushrooms, fresh or dried (& soaked) shiitake or stone mushrooms, sliced

200 g leaf spinach, fresh, cleaned

1 bunch of spring onion(s), cut into 5 cm long pieces

½ Head Chinese cabbage, cut into bite-sized pieces

For the rear:

¾ cup/s of soy sauce

¾ cup/s of sake, (Japanese rice wine) or white wine

5 tablespoons of sugar

½ cup/s of fish broth - dashi (1 pinch of instant fish broth dissolved in 0.5 cup of water) - alternatively strongly diluted Gem

Oil, for frying

4 eggs

Preparation

Mix the ingredients for the stock and bring to the boil briefly.

Arrange meat and vegetables on a serving dish.

Place Rechaud on the table with a low saucepan or pan, add oil. When the oil is hot, add the meat and vegetables little by little and deglaze with the stock. Eat the cooked meat and vegetables and add the ingredients and stock to the pot again and again. Traditionally, the ingredients are briefly dipped in raw egg before eating - but this is not necessary!

Rice is served with it.

Sukiyaki is a typical winter meal and is always prepared directly at the table.

Beer and rice wine are particularly suitable as drinks.

SESAME CREAM WITH SUGAR SYRUP

Working time approx. 20 minutes
Rest period approx. 3 hours
cooking / baking time approx. 5 minutes
Total time approx. 3 hours 25 minutes

ingredients
500 g milk
3 tablespoons of sugar
80 g sesame
3 ½ Gelatine leaf
Also: (for the syrup)
2 tablespoons sugar, brown
4 tablespoons sugar, white
100 ml water

Preparation
Roast the sesame seeds in a pan without oil. Put a spoon aside, purée the rest to a paste, preferably with a corn mill or alternatively with a hand

blender. You can also buy ready-made sesame paste. If you want to use it, it should contain only sesame seeds without oil and spices.

Stir the paste in the milk, add 3 tablespoons of sugar and heat until the sugar has dissolved. Stir the sesame paste evenly. Soak the gelatine in a little cold water, squeeze it and mix it in the hot but not boiling sesame milk. Pour into small bowls and leave to stiffen in the refrigerator for a few hours.

For the syrup, heat the two types of sugar in water until everything has dissolved. Let it cool down. Scatter the sesame seeds set aside on the sesame cream and pour on the sugar syrup to serve.

JAPANESE SEAWEED SALAD

Working time approx. 10 minutes
Rest period approx. 1 hour
cooking / baking time approx. 10 minutes
Total time approx. 1 hour 20 minutes

ingredients
1 bag of Wakame, dried seaweed (one bag contains 56 grams)
3 tablespoons vinegar, (sushi, rice)
3 tablespoons sesame oil
1 tablespoon lime juice
1 tablespoon ginger, freshly grated
1 tablespoon of sugar
1 clove/n garlic, pressed
2 tablespoons coriander green, finely chopped
½ tablespoon chili powder
1 tablespoon sesame

Preparation
Pour hot water over seaweed and leave to soak for 10 minutes.

Prepare the sauce:
mix all the above ingredients (except the seaweed and sesame seeds) in a small bowl until smooth. Season to taste with the chili powder according to the desired spiciness.

Drain the seaweed and wring out a little. Now simply fold the drained seaweed into the sauce and sprinkle sesame seeds over it as desired. Leave to soak for about 1 hour, preferably in the refrigerator.

The wakame salad can also be frozen in portions.

BAKED CHICKEN WITH JAPANESE SAUCE

Total time approx. 15 minutes

ingredients
400 g chicken breast
1 egg, whisked
½ cup potato flour (or other starch flour)
Oil

For the sauce:
1 cup of broth (Dashi, 1 teaspoon of instant fish broth dissolved in 1 cup of water, alternatively 1 cup strongly diluted
1 tablespoon of sugar
4 tablespoons sake, white wine or mild sherry
4 tablespoons soy sauce, Japanese

Preparation
Cut the chicken breast into bite-sized pieces. Then dip the pieces first in the beaten egg mixture and then turn them in potato flour.

Mix the ingredients for the sauce well in a bowl. Heat oil in a pan and fry the meat pieces on both sides until golden brown. Pour the sauce evenly over the meat pieces. Simmer over medium heat for about 5 minutes until the sauce thickens.

MAKI

Total time approx. 45 minutes

Ingredients
250 g rice, (sushi rice)
375 ml water
1 tablespoon rice vinegar
½ Tablespoon Mirin
½ tablespoon sugar
1 teaspoon of salt
6 Nori leaves
250 g salmon steak, fried in the pan from both sides for 8 minutes each and cut into strips
1 teaspoon wasabi paste
6 cm cucumber(s), with skin, cut into thin strips
½ Pepper(s), red, cut into thin strips

Preparation
Wash the rice in a sieve under running water until the draining water is clear. Bring the rice and the water in a pot quickly to a boil, reduce the heat considerably and cook the rice for 10-12 minutes. In the meantime, mix the rice vinegar with mirin, sugar and salt in a small bowl until everything is completely dissolved. Put the rice in a flat bowl (no

metal!) and let it cool down for 10 minutes. Add the rice vinegar solution and carefully fold it in with a wooden spoon. Allow to cool completely and divide into 6 portions of equal size.

Now place a nori leaf on a bamboo mat, shiny side down, and spread 1 portion of rice thinly and evenly on top; leave a 1.5 cm margin at one end. Make a furrow in the front third with a spoon handle across the rolling direction and spread wasabi paste in it. Be careful, wasabi is quite hot! Then put the fried salmon strips into the furrow and put cucumber and/or paprika strips behind it as desired. Moisten the free end of the nori leaf with some water. Now lift the bamboo mat in front a little bit and lift the nori leaf around the filling under gentle pressure. Lift the bamboo mat further and continue to roll the sushi roll until it is completely closed. You have to practice this a few times. But with me it worked quite well the first time! Repeat this with the remaining 5 nori leaves.

At the end there are 6 nice sushi rolls in front of you and wait for the final maki shape. Now you have to prepare the tool first, that means to make a good knife ultra sharp(!). Otherwise the Maki-Sushi look more like car tires! Put a sushi roll on a wooden board and cut the ends cleanly straight (the rest is for the cook!). Dip the knife into cold water again and again before each further cutting! Divide the sushi roll in the middle and cut each half into 4 equal maki sushi. Arrange them on a large plate with the cut surface facing upwards. Put the finished Sushi in a cool place or eat it immediately.

FRIED UDON NOODLES WITH BEEF

Working time approx. 20 minutes
cooking / baking time approx. 8 minutes
Total time approx. 28 minutes

ingredients
200 g Udon noodles
130 g beef, cut into thin slices
1 handful of bean sprouts
1 handful of Chinese cabbage, cut into strips
5 g Mu-Err mushrooms, dried
1 garlic clove(s), chopped
2 slice/s of ginger root, chopped
1 shallot(s), chopped
1 tablespoon oyster sauce
some salt and pepper

Preparation
Pour boiling water over the Mu-Err mushrooms, let them soak and cut into strips.

Pour boiling water over the udon noodles as well and let them stand for 2 - 3 minutes until they are soft and you can get them apart.

Fry the chopped garlic and ginger together with the shallot in a little oil for a short time and then add the thin strips of beef, fry very briefly, add the Mu-Err mushrooms and season with a little salt. Immediately after that, fry the noodles for a short time and then add the Chinese cabbage, the soy sprouts, the soy sauce, the oyster sauce and 2-3 tablespoons of water, season with salt and pepper to taste and continue frying for a very short time.

CHICKEN TERIYAKI

Working time approx. 25 minutes
Rest period approx. 2 minutes
cooking / baking time approx. 20 minutes
Total time approx. 47 minutes

ingredients
4 tablespoons soy sauce
4 tablespoons rice wine, mirin or sake
2 tablespoons of sugar
1 teaspoon ginger, fresh, grated
1 teaspoon garlic, finely chopped
¼ teaspoon chili flakes, optional
1 teaspoon sesame, peeled
4 chicken legs with skin, boneless
1 teaspoon of cornstarch
salt and pepper
1 spring onion(s), cut diagonally into very thin rings
250 g broccoli florets, steamed, lightly salted and peppered
1 teaspoon sesame oil
Rice, cooked

Preparation
Whisk soy sauce, rice wine and sugar in a bowl. The

original Teriyaki recipe does not include ginger, garlic or chili flakes, but I like the taste very much.

Rinse chicken legs under cold water, pat dry, add a little salt and pepper on both sides (you can leave it alone, the soy sauce in the marinade also provides salt). Then sprinkle very thinly with cornflour and rub it lightly into the meat.

In a coated pan, lightly roast the sesame seeds without fat at medium heat while stirring frequently until they are tenderly golden brown. Pour into a small bowl and put aside.

Now heat the pan well, put the Pollo fino with the skin side down in the pan. Turn the heat down to medium heat (for me level 6 or 7 of 9) and fry the meat until the skin is golden brown (approx. 6 - 7 minutes). Turn the meat over and fry on the other side as well. After another 5 - 6 minutes, the meat is also cooked inside. Remove from the pan and remove the fat from the pan as completely as possible using kitchen paper.

Whisk the marinade again briefly and add it to the pan (medium heat!). Breathe in deeply and enjoy the aroma! Add the Pollo fino to the marinade. Let it simmer until it is significantly reduced and caramelized and has the desired saucy consistency. Turn the meat several times and spoon the marinade over it again and again, so that it is covered all around by the shiny sauce. If the sauce thickens too much, you can carefully dilute it by the spoonful with a little water.

Turn off the stove. Lift the Pollo fino out of the sauce, let it drip off just above the pan, rest on a board with the crispy skin facing upwards for 1-2 minutes.

Meanwhile, arrange the rice and broccoli on plates. Add a few drops of sesame oil to the broccoli. Then cut the meat with a very sharp knife crosswise into 1 - 2 cm wide strips. Drape it on or next to the rice. Drizzle with the remaining sauce, garnish with the spring onion rings and sesame seeds and enjoy!

JAPANESE GRILLED SALMON WITH TERIYAKI SAUCE

400 kcal
Total time approx. 30 minutes

ingredients
4 salmon steak (approx. 250g each)
For the sauce:
2 teaspoons of sugar
2 tablespoons sake (Japanese rice wine), alternatively white wine or mild sherry
2 tablespoons rice wine, Mirin (Japanese sweet rice wine for cooking - available in the Asia Shop)
4 tablespoons soy sauce, jap.
1 pack of cress
15 cm radish, white (grated)
Oil, for frying

Preparation

Dab the salmon chops and if possible remove skin and middle bones. (Caution! Chops must not fall apart!)

For the teriyaki sauce, mix all ingredients, up to and including the soy sauce, until the sugar has dissolved. (Works best when the ingredients are slightly warmed up).

Marinate the fish in the sauce for about 10 minutes. Turn frequently.

Wash and drain the cress and grate the radish.

When preparing on the (electric) grill:
Drain the fish a little (but keep the marinade!) and put it on the grill. Grill each side for about 3 minutes, brushing with the marinade from time to time.

When preparing the fish in the pan:
Heat some oil in the pan, then fry the fish for about 3 minutes on each side.

Pour off any excess oil and add the rest of the marinade to the pan. Bring to the boil and let the fish simmer in the sauce for a few more minutes.

Divide the salmon into 4 plates and pour over the roast stock or the rest of the marinade. Garnish with cress and grated radish.

Serve with rice and salad!

JAPANESE NOODLE SOUP WITH CHICKEN BROTH AND SIRLOIN - RAMEN

Working time approx. 45 minutes
cooking / baking time approx. 5 hours
Total time approx. 5 hours 45 minutes

ingredients
1 pork fillet in one piece, approx. 500 g
1 soup chicken (also deep-frozen)
1 piece ginger root, approx. 8 cm
water at will
100 ml soy sauce, Japanese
100 ml rice wine or sake
500 g soup noodles
4 clove/s of garlic
1 stick/s of leek

4 carrot(s)
1 nori leaves
100 g bean sprouts, fresh
3 eggs
3 spring onion(s)
salt and pepper
1 tablespoon of sugar

Preparation
The broth:
Place the soup chicken in cold water with a stick of leek, one onion, three to four cloves of garlic, five centimeters of ginger in one piece, pinch of salt, three to four carrots and a handful of seaweed (optional). Add enough water to cover the chicken completely. (Choose the pot size so that everything plus two to three liters of water will fit in well - a five liter pot is quite ideal).

Slowly bring to the boil and simmer for at least 3 - 4 hours. The broth is even more delicious with cooking times of 6 - 8 hours. If there is foam, you can skim it off, but you don't have to. The broth should not boil too much - just simmer lightly. The longer this broth boils, the better. Then strain the broth.

It is worth using a good and above all real soup chicken or fresh chicken. If you take a chicken, after about 1 hour of cooking time you can completely remove the meat from the bones and let everything but the meat (bone, cartilage, skin) continue to simmer in the broth. You can prepare many other dishes from the meat (e.g. Thai chicken salad and much more).

The loin:
Sear the pork loin in a pan briefly from all sides until it is slightly browned. Do not fry it too long - just brown it lightly! Then place it in a pan and pour 100 ml of soy sauce (I use Kikkoman because it is naturally brewed) and 50 to 100 ml of rice wine (I use Chinese rice wine). Add 1 tablespoon of sugar, a sliced spring onion (with the green and only a little of the onion) and 3 cm of grated fresh ginger. Pour a little water over it so that the loin is almost completely covered with liquid. Then bring the liquid to a boil. Again, let it simmer only slightly.

After 40 minutes, remove the loin from the liquid and put it aside. Then cut the loin into slices of approx. 2 - 3 mm before adding it to the soup.

The loin should come from a good butcher - there are amazing differences in quality. A good loin after this procedure is very tender and juicy and not tough and dry.

The eggs:
Hard boil four eggs and peel them. Add the eggs to the loin stock and simmer for 10 minutes. Turn them again and again so that they are evenly browned by the broth. When they are done, halve them and put them aside.

The noodles:
You can make your own noodles while the broth is boiling (recipes are in the database) or use Chinese noodles from Asiashop. I have made quite good experiences with Quick-Noodles, but even spaghetti tastes very good in them. If you have a well-assorted asian store, you might even get Ramen Noodles or fresh Ramen Noodles. But always cook the noodles strictly according to instructions and rather too hard than too soft.

The soup:
When the chicken broth is ready, put it in a pot together with the loin broth and season with a few tablespoons of soy sauce and another small shot of rice wine. Possibly add more salt, but actually the soy sauce should provide enough salt. Then bring everything to the boil again. You can also add more water, depending on how much or how diluted you want the soup to be. I leave the broth pure without adding water. When the soup boils, all other ingredients should be ready for the next step, especially the noodles.

The garnish:
Scald the bean sprouts with hot water in a sieve. Cut the green of two spring onions into rings. Cut small strips (about 2 x 3 cm) from the nori leaves.

The finish:
Pour the soup into a bowl and add as many noodles

that the noodles reach just below the surface.

Place two to three slices of sirloin on top. You can sprinkle some more coarse pepper on the sirloin.

Place half an egg with the yolk facing upwards on the edge of the bowl.

Sprinkle a small handful of sprouts and spring onions on top and then add the nori leaf.

Enjoy the sight of the soup, preferably eating with chopsticks and slurp the broth loudly - then it tastes best.

O - YAKODON

Total time approx. 30 minutes

ingredients
200 ml water
45 ml soy sauce, dark, Japanese
45 ml Sake (Mirin), sweet
1 teaspoon of sugar
½ Package ready mix (daship powder)
2 chicken breasts
4 eggs
2 onion(s)
300 g rice (round grain rice)

Preparation
Bring the water to a boil in a large pot. Add the dashi powder (fish sauce powder), soy sauce, sugar and the mirin (cooking sake). Cut the chicken into slices and add to the simmering broth. Cut onions into rings and add them.

While the meat is cooking, take a bowl and beat the eggs into it. Do not stir. Tear open with chopsticks. Dip the open chopsticks again and again, close the chopsticks and pull them up. The eggs should be mixed a little bit like a thread pattern (if not, it is not too bad).

Now pour the eggs into the pot in a circle and do not stir. Put the lid on the pot and turn up the heat so that it boils well. Cook for about 2 - 3 minutes until the eggs are firm. Divide the cooked rice into bowls and spread the donburi (with broth) on top.

ICHIGO DAIFUKU

Working time approx. 1 hour
cooking / baking time approx. 4 minutes
Total time approx. 1 hour 4 minutes

ingredients
1 ½ Cup/s of flour (glutinous flour)
1 cup of water
½ cup of sugar
1 tin of paste (Anko, sweet red bean paste)
10 strawberries
Starch flour, to flour the hands

Preparation
Wash and clean 10 strawberries and coat them with a thin layer of Anko. Small strawberries are best.

Mix flour, sugar and water in a microwaveable container until everything is lump-free. Put the lid on top and put it in the microwave for about 4 minutes at the highest setting.
When the dough is slightly transparent and has the consistency of an earlobe, it is ready. Otherwise, put it back in the microwave for a few seconds.

Flour a board with starch and put the dough on it,

dust the surface again.

Cut the dough into equally sized pieces with a moistened knife. Be careful, the dough is very sticky.

Press the dough flat, put the strawberry anko ball inside and close the dough around it.

Press the edges together carefully. The result should be a closed ball.

Results in 10 balls.

CRISPY CHICKEN SCHNITZEL WITH CURRY SAUCE

Working time approx. 30 minutes
cooking / baking time approx. 30 minutes
Total time approx. 1 hour

ingredients
For the schnitzels:
4 chicken breasts
Sea salt and pepper, black
Flour for flour milling
2 eggs
Panko
Sunflower oil for baking

For the sauce: (curry sauce)
2 tablespoons sunflower oil
1 large onion(s)
2 clove(s) of garlic
1 piece ginger, walnut-sized
1 as desired Chilli pepper(s)

1 tablespoon, heaped flour
3 teaspoons curry powder, mild
1 teaspoon Garam Masala
1 tablespoon rice vinegar, alternatively apple vinegar
3 tablespoons soy sauce
2 tablespoons honey
1 large carrot(s)
1 bell pepper(s), red
1 apple
150 ml apple juice
400 ml chicken broth
1 teaspoon, heaped cornstarch

For the side dish:
4 portions of jasmine rice, cooked

Preparation
For the curry sauce, finely dice the onion, chop the garlic and ginger finely and cut the chili pepper into thin rings. Cut the carrot, the bell pepper and the apple into small cubes.

Heat two tablespoons of sunflower oil in a saucepan and sauté the onion in it until transparent. Add a heaped tablespoon of flour and fry over medium heat for about 4 minutes, stirring continuously. Add garlic, ginger, chili, curry powder and Garam Masala and fry briefly. Deglaze with the rice vinegar and soy sauce. Then add the honey, finely diced carrot, bell pepper, apple, apple juice and chicken stock. Cook everything for 15 to 20 minutes at medium heat. Finally, add the starch dissolved in cold water to bind the curry sauce and bring to the boil briefly. Season to taste with salt and pepper.

Cut the chicken breast in half horizontally with a sharp knife and season with salt and pepper. Build a breading line with one plate of flour, the beaten eggs and the panko. Turn the chicken escalopes on both sides first in the flour, then in the egg and finally in the panko and tap them off.

Heat plenty of sunflower oil in a pan and fry the escalopes one after the other at medium to high heat until golden brown on both sides. Place the finished cutlets on kitchen paper to drain and then place them in the oven preheated to 80 °C top/bottom heat to keep them warm.

Cut the escalopes diagonally into strips about one centimeter wide. Serve with curry sauce and cooked jasmine rice.

ANPAN

Working time approx. 10 minutes
Rest period approx. 1 hour
Total time approx. 1 hour 10 minutes

ingredients
450 g flour
2 tablespoons of sugar
200 ml water
20 g yeast
40 g butter
1 egg, separated
1 pinch(s) of salt
150 g spice paste, (sweet red bean paste, Anko, alternatively Nutella)

Preparation
Put flour, sugar, salt, egg white and butter in a bowl. Dissolve the yeast in lukewarm water, gradually add it to the ingredients and knead everything into a smooth yeast dough. Cover the dough and let it rise in a warm place for 30 minutes.

Then divide the dough into 10 equal pieces, press each one a little bit flat and put a spoon of Anko or

Nutella on the middle of each. Close the edges over the filling so that you get 10 dough balls. Place the balls with enough space between them on a baking tray lined with baking paper, brush them with some water, cover them with a towel and let them rise for another 20 minutes in a warm place.

Whisk the egg yolk and brush the Anpan with it. Bake for 15 minutes at 180°C convection oven. Let cool down.

UDON NOODLES WITH TOFU AND SPINACH IN PEPPER SAUCE

Working time approx. 20 minutes
cooking / baking time approx. 20 minutes
Total time approx. 40 minutes

ingredients
2 handfuls of baby spinach
270 g Udon noodles
200 g tofu
1 tablespoon sesame
some sesame oil

For the sauce:
50 ml water
6 tablespoons soy sauce
3 tablespoons rice vinegar
2 tablespoons cornstarch
1 tablespoon of pepper

3 teaspoons garlic granules
2 teaspoons agave syrup
1 teaspoon ginger powder

Preparation

For the pepper sauce, dissolve the starch in cold water. Add the soy sauce, rice wine vinegar, ginger, agave syrup, garlic and pepper and blend to a smooth sauce.

Bring the water to the boil and cook the noodles for 4 - 5 minutes until they are firm to the bite. Drain the noodles and rinse them with cold water to prevent them from sticking together.

Cut the tofu into cubes. Heat some sesame oil in a larger pan and fry the tofu until the cubes are brown all around. Remove the pan from the heat, deglaze with a dash of water, add a dash of pepper sauce and toss the pan through once so that the tofu is glazed all around. Put the tofu aside.

Add some sesame oil to the already used pan. When the oil is hot, add the noodles and the pepper sauce. Fry the noodles while stirring constantly until they are cooked and completely covered with sauce. Remove the pan from the heat and stir in the spinach and diced tofu.

Divide the noodles between 4 plates and serve garnished with sesame seeds.

IMPRINT

Mindful Publishing

by
TTENTION Inc.
Wilmington - DE19806
Trolley Square 20c

All rights reserved

Instagram: mindful_publishing
Contact: mindful.publishing@web.de

Manufactured by Amazon.ca
Bolton, ON